RASCUACHA TECH

A digital resistance roadmap for justice and autonomy

By Iris Rodriguez

XICANA CHRONICLES

With great humility and thanks,

I offer these flowers of my experience to the universe.

In memory of Anthony "Zin" Mills aka Wali Aqueem

TABLE OF CONTENTS

ACKNOWLEDGEMENTS

I want to give special thanks to all those who have walked with me through the digital landscape over the last 13 years. I want to thank my children, my partner, and my parents for helping me reach this milestone. I want to thank my friends, and relatives who have inspired and supported me in big and small ways: Cynthia Lawson, Hollie Peterson, Yvette Mendez, Virginia Raymond, Laura Perez, LC Johnson, Tonatzin Roman, Viva Flores, Celeste De Luna, Anayanse Garza, Rebecca Flores, Esther Portillo-Gonzalez, Laura Rios Ramirez, Luissana Santibañez, Madelein Santibañez, Rosario Martinez, T.E.J.A.S., Martina Cartwright, Juan Parras, Bryan Parras, Liana Lopez, Roberto Dr. Cintli Rodriguez, Dr. Lorenzo Cano, Rosa Tupina Yaotonalcuauhtli, Esther Salinas, Eva Martinez, and Heriberto and Georgina Rodriguez.

And last but not least, a big THANK YOU to the supporters of the Xicana Chronicles publishing house campaign that contributed directly to the publication of this book:

Homies

Josefa M Molina / Juan Tejeda/Aztlan Libre Press

Comadres / Compadres / Compas

Anselmo C Cruz / Armando E Bernal / LC Johnson / Mona Alvarado Frazier Tonantzin Society / Yvette Mendez

Shout Out

Lea Arellano (Two Spirit Medicine / Human Solutions) / Rebecca Flores / Deborah Gallegos / Julian Lopez / Glenn Robinson / Tonatzin Roman

INTRODUCTION

This book was written to assist communities of color in the U.S. who have mobilized to assert autonomy and demand justice, specifically those who experience ongoing trauma, lack of economic resources, media blackout, backlash from the non-profit industrial complex, technological divides, and other communication barriers.

In this text I document my thirteen-year journey as a digital warrior and rascuacha tech. During my journey through the digital world, I have served as an organizer, multimedia producer, and digital resistance warrior in community-led campaigns on issues including environmental justice, family detention, decolonization, cultural arts, guerrilla media, Xicanisma, and public archives. In 2012, I founded Xica Media, a Xicana-powered multimedia, multilingual digital resistance network that runs six channels, including Xica Nation, Xicana Chronicles, End Family Detention, Mission Texas Coalition, Tezcatlipoca Records, and Yetlanezi. These networks have a collective following in over 120 countries and reach all age brackets.

Given the increasing fascism and corporate control of media and information in the U.S., I felt a need to share my experiences so that communities seeking justice and autonomy can save valuable time and resources as they assert digital power. Because I believe that stories have the power to change the world, I am sharing my own story in hopes that it too can make a difference.

I will warn you now that this book is not written in perfect English. I use non-traditional spellings for certain terms and my voice may shift as I switch topics and genres. My lens is radical and based on my experience as an 80s kid and Xicana from Texas. I approached this text as a written interview and outlined my digital visions in the form of question and answer.

What I offer is not an end-all solution or social-justice-in-a-box. In this text are stories, opinions, recurring themes, and lessons learned from my digital warpath that I hope will help community-led movements for justice and autonomy. The text is broken into four parts: Definitions, Reflections, Inside the Machine, and Things to Consider.

In the spirit of resistance and love, I offer these flowers of my experience to the world. These are the virtual arrows of the digital warrior. They must be used carefully to defend, create, liberate, and heal.

PART I: DEFINITIONS

CHAPTER 1: DEFINING DIGITAL RESISTANCE

What is digital resistance?

Digital resistance is the use of technology and multimedia to create internet-based front lines to support community-led movements for justice and autonomy.

The three primary functions of digital resistance are to:

- **document** first-hand experiences,
- **digitize** information, and
- **disseminate** information across the digital world.

For the purposes of this text, we will explore digital resistance from within the framework of rascuacha tech, which is a method that can be applied to digital resistance in order to create resource-friendly informational, ideological, and participatory web-based tools to support community-led campaigns.

What is digital resistance not?

Digital resistance is not a stand-alone approach to obtain justice or assert autonomy. It is not static and evolves with technology and standards of internet governance. Digital resistance is not social-justice-in-a-box or an "easy fix." It is not a one-size-fits-all solution to community issues. Digital resistance cannot be defined strictly by my terms or my opinions. I am merely a witness to the power of digital resistance and rascuacha tech.

Whom should digital resistance benefit?

Digital resistance should benefit and be directly organized by the community experiencing the injustice. However, advocates and activists can come together with the community to maintain a strong digital war front and support the movement on the ground.

How are digital resistance, advocacy, and activism related?

Digital resistance exists only when members from the community at the center of the struggle lead a web-based effort to support the movement on the ground. Those that are not part of the community at the center can act in solidarity. A digital resistance movement can include the participation of activists and advocates.

What are the most common forms of digital resistance?

The most common forms of digital resistance include websites, social media pages, and e-petitions. There are many other forms of digitized first-hand experiences that can be used as part of a digital resistance effort. These include news articles, voice recordings, radio, videos, photographs, art, scanned PDFs, publicly shared documents, and others. This definition will expand as new technologies are developed.

Why is access to technology a privilege?

While many Americans see cell phones and internet usage as commonplace, there are still many communities within the U.S. and the rest of the world that do not have the same relationship with technology. Many people still do not engage in or have access to the internet or the same sophisticated technological tools that we consider commonplace. It boils down to class, economics, culture, generation, and access.

We as a digitized generation have an unprecedented amount of power that the generations before us did not have. We have the privilege of being able to communicate instantly with the world through the internet. We also have the privilege of crafting our own narratives into digital codices that can never be burned.

Access to technology is a privilege and a powerful tool of positive change.

How can folks with these privileges help?

- Share tech skills with the community. This could mean conducting a skills share meeting or an informal presentation at home.

- Help spread the word online about the movement via a post on social media, joining a hashtag conversation about the issue, or using some other digital avenue to promote the voices of those at the center.
- Connect the community movement to your social networks and vice versa.
- Ask the community how you can help aid their efforts online.
- Have a conversation with your close friends and trusted family about the community struggle. Bring the issue home.

Who should be involved in digital resistance and why?

Digital resistance exists when members of a community-led movement for justice and autonomy use multimedia and the internet to create a web-based front line to support the movement on the ground.

There is room for solidarity from everyone in the digital movement. Every individual and every action in the virtual world has the power to influence and effect positive change on a global scale. It is through acts of solidarity by a mass number of individuals that virality and positive social change are possible in a digital resistance movement. Everyone should get involved.

Who should not be involved and why?

The power of digital resistance belongs to the community at the center. Individuals who are not members of the community at the center of the struggle must be permitted by the community to participate. Paid and unpaid individuals and organizations can contribute to digital resistance movements by acting in solidarity with the community-led movement.

There is something to be said for social justice organizing from sources that do not have vested financial interests in the existence of a community's suffering.

What are the first steps to start a digital resistance movement?

If you are part of a community-led movement and are wanting to construct a web-based front line to support the movement on the ground, you can start from where you are with what you've got.

- Take stock of all technological tools available to document and digitize first-hand experiences. For example, if the only thing available is a camera, you can use it to take pictures or video and upload them to social media. Or if the only tool available is a phone, there are free ways (such as using Skype or Blog Talk Radio) to set-up call-in numbers to record stories or conversations by phone.

- Get informed about the issue from all sides. It is important to gain an understanding of the PR strategies and social stigmas that work against the movement. A stronger strategical vision for the digital resistance war front can be created by taking the time to understand the perspectives and speaking points of the opposing party, the media, paid actors, government contractors, or non-profits involved in the issue.

- Talk to folks within the community of all ages about the issue.

- Assess the communication flow about the issue within the community. Is the present flow of communication to the benefit or detriment of the movement?

- Expand your skills. Take a few moments out of your day or week to learn how to do something new online that can be applied to supporting the movement. There are tons of free tutorials online that can teach you website design, graphic design, layout, social media, and other tech skills. Expanding your abilities further strengthens the pool of resources the movement can draw from.

Why is skills sharing important?

Skills sharing is important because it provides a direct way to close historical, intergenerational, linguistic, or technological divides. It also serves to decentralize and redistribute power in a circular way. The sharing of skills, perspectives, and stories can help provide a stronger ideological and logistical base for implementing digital strategies.

Why are first-hand experiences important?

Documenting, digitizing, and disseminating the first-hand experiences of historically oppressed communities are acts of resistance that take a stand against the intergenerational campaign of burning and banning our histories. These three acts allow communities in struggle to write their own histories and share first-hand experiences in real time, a power which preceding generations did not have.

The core product of digital resistance is a communal construction of a free, perpetual, public, multimedia, and infinitely shareable first-hand historical archive. With everyday tools, we have the power to construct our own sets of virtual codices, ones which can never be burned.

How do nonprofits relate to digital resistance?

Non-profit organizations are not the end-all, save-all for justice movements. Some were born out of community suffering and others profit from it. I know of cases where the leaders of the non-profit are local folks with deep roots in the community. I have witnessed the healing work they do. I also know non-profits involved in social issues as paid community outsiders and third-party government contractors. I have seen them compete with the community-led resistance movements for resources, media attention, and control the public narrative for local and national news. In digital resistance, the community-led movement ultimately decides what role nonprofits play.

How do government agencies relate to community-led resistance movements?

Communities of color in the U.S. know all too well that the same veils of multiple marginalities that apply to society (sexism, racism, classism, xenophobia, etc.) also apply to government agencies. Using the EPA as an example, "Superfund Sites" in communities of color go unaddressed or only partially addressed. Many of these communities are left out of critical conversations around remediation and resolution altogether.

While approaching these agencies can be part of a strategy to obtain relief and justice, placing full faith in a broken system will not yield positive results, no matter how helpful the title of the agency may seem.

What is exponentiality and why is it important?

"Exponentiality" is one way to reach the third goal of digital resistance - to disseminate information. Exponentiality can manifest through planning and executing a multimedia, multiplatform dissemination strategy. With a lack of money, time, energy, or volunteers, the workflow has to be streamlined while setup to reach as many audiences as possible. There are many ways to achieve this. Web site posts could be set to automatically share links across social media upon being published. Posts could be optimized to always include links to relevant websites or hashtags in the content. Also using as many forms of multimedia as possible will help reach and create new audiences.

WordPress offers automated republishing of new posts to certain social media platforms through a plugin called Jetpack. There are other tools such as Hootsuite that may help extend this automation even further. However, if these are not possible, manually re-posting links across social media still works, although it can be time-consuming.

What are the top three mistakes to avoid in digital resistance?

- Not optimizing or automating processes.
  With resources at a minimum, efficiency is key. Finding and creating ways to automate processes can save time and person power.
- Not curating information in an organized, accessible, or searchable way. There are many ways to display information. Getting feedback on usability and auditing website statistics are two ways to determine if the placement and dissemination of content need to be reconsidered.
- Not protecting the mind, body, and spirit.
  The virtual world is directly connected to the spiritual world and the physical world. Digital warriors should protect themselves at all levels.

CHAPTER 2: DEFINING RASCUACHA TECH

For me, rascuacha tech has been a survival-based, economically-challenged ingenuity born out of the barrio that consists of creatively fusing multiple free (or low cost) technologies to assert digital power. I also use the term to describe my body of work. I use the term "rascuacha" but in no way do I believe this concept is exclusive to any gender. I am sure it could be just as rascuachx, rascuacho, and rascuache.

Rascuacha tech is fluid and constantly evolving. It can be applied to different circumstances and resource considerations. It changes over time with the development of technology and digital trends.

By applying rascuacha tech to digital resistance, informational, ideological, and participatory tools can be created (using minimal resources) to support community-led movements for justice and autonomy. Injustice can be exposed, public awareness can be raised, direct action can be stimulated, first-hand historical narratives can be created and shared in real-time, and a global audience can be reached.

I will briefly describe the philosophy and application of rascuacha tech from my perspective.

Philosophy of rascuacha tech

Within digital resistance, rascuacha tech is a survival-based, economically-challenged tech ingenuity that has the power to change the world. It has the power to reach between the physical, virtual, and spiritual realms.

Rascuacha tech requires a strong spiritual vision in order to manifest beyond virtual and physical borders and limitations. It requires some emotional resilience to practice a tactical culture of creativity and creation in the face of ongoing oppression, racism, sexism, money issues, etc. Rascuacha tech sees technological and material obstacles as opportunities to apply ingenuity and create resource-friendly solutions and workarounds.

Using rascuacha tech for digital resistance

The following list contains examples of tactical applications of rascuacha tech in digital resistance:

- Digitizing first-hand experiences using many forms of multimedia (through audio recording, video, pictures, document scans, etc.) to quilt a multidimensional narrative and stimulate the senses.
- Avoiding legal issues and other costs by utilizing the element of surprise to collect or disseminate first-hand experiences and other information.
- Using undercover operations, such as:
- Dressing and speaking in ways to blend with the dominant culture to access spaces of power with minimal suspicion of infiltration.
- Using professional-looking (yet homemade) media badges to access spaces of power.
- Projecting authority through posture and presence.
- Taking advantage of public events and spaces to collect content and share information.
- Using underground or street culture to connect, create, and disseminate information.
- Repeating creative hashtags or slogans in all communications to facilitate name recognition.
- Establishing a routine of communication dissemination.
- Finding free alternatives to create online communities and share information to as large an audience as possible.

What are the top rascuacha tech techniques you have used?

The path of the digital warrior is not easy. It is difficult to be under attack. The path of the digital warrior requires one to battle outwardly and inwardly. Resources may be scarce and there may not be much time to take action on an issue. But if something inside you refuses to give in, that feeling should be honored. The most profound lessons we learn come from overcoming hardships.

As I mentioned earlier, my journey in digital resistance was born in blood and fire. The techniques below come from the many mistakes and lessons I learned over the last thirteen years. I share these with love in the hopes that they help save a movement time, money, and energy. Here are the top techniques I have used in my journey as a digital warrior:

Technology as a tool of positive change

It is a privilege to have access to technology and technological knowledge. We as a digitized generation are able to connect with people across the globe in seconds. The power we hold in our hands is unparalleled in human history. It has changed the way we communicate and connect as human beings. Within the realm of digital resistance, technology is used to assert virtual power to effect positive change by moving a mass number of individual hearts to action through a computer screen.

Undercover operations

Digitized content can include first-hand experiences or other documents with relevant information. In those times when it is necessary to obtain information not freely shared with the community, going undercover to investigate the matter further can produce interesting results. Successful undercover operations (or infiltrations) consist of accessing a space of power in person by blending in within the dominant culture in order to collect or disseminate information. Some tactics I have used in the past that have worked for me include:

- Dressing and talking "white." When necessary, I did my best to appear assimilated, speaking with a mainstream American accent, using English pronunciations of Spanish words.
- Using homemade media badges, making them look as professional as possible.
- Projecting authority through posture and presence. For example, sitting and walking with my back straight and shoulders square. I also made it a point to limit my facial expressions and hand gestures.

Pooling resources

There is room for everybody in the movement. Do not assume that just because an individual has or does not have a college degree or a fancy job that they lack vision or ability. The solidarity of individuals from all walks of life is necessary. Do not discourage the elders or the non-techie folks from participating; they may have visions that can help guide the movement in directions that were previously unconsidered. Brainstorming and being open to ideas from all directions will result in a broader strategic vision and outreach campaign. Also include folks that can help pray or send positive thoughts toward the movement. All positive energies are needed, especially when combating an enemy with deep pockets, political power, and the power to move abstract energies like ignorance and greed through corporate media.

It is imperative that resources be pooled to circumvent any individual/communal disadvantages. Everybody has something to contribute and if everybody gives a little, together you can go a very long way. Through the collective effort, change is possible.

Go rascuachx

Energy, time, and money are luxuries. You should use what you have and start where you are. Do not be ashamed if resources are low. Do not let any self-defeating thought stop you from taking action. Think in terms of exponentiality in order to maximize efficiency and resources from the start. Take advantage of free networks and services and integrate them into the digital war front. But if this is not possible, simply do the best with what you have.

Multimedia multiplatform, multilingual

There are different ways to create a site like the one I describe for little to no cost. Remember that the wider an audience you aim for, the greater your chances are of going viral. Set your sights beyond the United States media. If possible, seek volunteers to help translate content to other languages. Automate publishing from the website to social media accounts to spread the message across platforms and networks with the push of one button.

Because the sharing of information is a form of active resistance, sorting your website so that it can simultaneously serve as a digital multimedia library is imperative. Creating a section for multimedia or downloadable resources is critical. Organizing information neatly and making it searchable arms your audience with the tools they need to learn more and take action immediately.

The two main objectives of the site are to raise awareness and move hearts to action. The more ways you evoke and communicate these on your virtual spaces, the greater the chances you can engage an audience who stands in solidarity with the movement.

Think outside the box

In the virtual universe, anything is possible. Look for new ways to reach a broader audience or make your work easier. Find creative and inclusive ways to plan, strategize, and improve the site. Think outside the box and beyond the borders. Dare to dream big.

Artist solidarity

The solidarity of visual and musical artists can take the digital war front to the next level. Yes, the layout and navigational structures of a site have to be easy to use. However, nowadays with social media, understanding how to attract the eye of a site visitor is its own science. Imagery plays a critical part of connecting people online. Expressing things visually in the virtual world is very effective because imagery communicates almost instantly.

Finding eye-catching images for content can be difficult because it requires the luxury of time, planning, or brainstorming. Or maybe the issue being conveyed on the website is very complicated and beyond the artistic ability of the digital warrior. Reaching out to the artist community can be a huge help as conveying complex themes visually is what they do best.

The collective effort makes the digital resistance war front more powerful. The movement becomes amplified by the contributions of each artist and their respective networks.

Digital libraries

There are certain elements of struggle that communities of color in the U.S. have in common. One of those is the lack of corporate media attention and public validation of our community issues. We know too well now that the corporate, white supremacist, patriarchal agenda of media networks can serve to silence, deny, or misrepresent the issues that affect our communities. By having a basic understanding of how to communicate information online, you can circumvent these things and create ways to connect directly with individuals around the world.

Creating a digital war front is one way to dismantle the media blackout. Instead of waiting for the media, become the media. By self-producing news, the movement can build networks to share information. It must make the organization of information navigable and easy to find. By sorting media and content by date, type, or genre, the audience becomes armed with tools that make searching and sharing easy.

Creating a digital record is an act of resistance. The moment it is published and comes to life, it can be infinitely shared, downloaded, or printed by anyone who obtains a web-based or remote digital copy. This means that anything that is birthed in the virtual universe has perpetual life. The fact that it can be downloaded and printed makes its very birth of threat to the oppressing party.

Creating and spreading virtual fires (virtual fire keeping)

A digital warrior is a virtual fire keeper. The position of a virtual fire keeper makes a digital warrior socially responsible. Be conscious of the type of fire you are spreading to people. The emotion evoked by a digital war front could incite positive or negative energies. Be mindful when putting out a stream of content that evokes sadness, hurt, pain, or suffering. Try to achieve some balance with the positive sides of the issue, those untold stories that inspire people to action. If you have too much negativity on a site, you might make your audience question why they should participate in the first place. You may also attract a certain type of audience that may not necessarily be good for the movement. However, if you are looking to build a site that engages people to take action, it needs to be more of a personality and more human in its range of emotions. It should be able to evoke as much inspiration and positivity as well as awareness of critical issues.

Self-care as resistance

Maintaining your physical, emotional, and spiritual well-being is an act of resistance. Making sure that your mind, body, and spirit are in optimal shape benefits you, your loved ones, and your community. Each link in the chain of family and community must be as strong as possible. Using ergonomic office supplies, creating a daily spiritual practice, and routinely grounding your bare feet on the earth are some examples of ways to care for yourself and reduce stress. I discuss this topic further in the last chapter of this book, Self-care as resistance.

PART II: REFLECTIONS

CHAPTER 3: BIRTH OF A DIGITAL WARRIOR

What forms of digital resistance do you participate in?

For the past thirteen years, I have served as an organizer, multimedia producer, and digital warrior in community-led campaigns for justice. I have worked on issues relating to environmental justice, ending family detention in the U.S., decolonization, cultural arts, guerrilla media, and public archives. I consider myself a rascuacha tech because I have an ability to engineer wide-reaching digital resistance platforms with minimal resources.

Currently, I continue to engage in digital resistance through contributing to groups such as the Texas Jail Project, Alma de Mujer Center for Social Change, and the Chinati Ixtlan Cultural Land Conservancy. I also run a series of digital resistance websites, projects, and social networks, including:

- XicaNation.com (decolonization)
- XicanaChronicles.com (writing or own herstories)
- EndFamilyDetention.com (ending family detention)
- Yetlanezi.com and TezcatlipocaRecords.com (preserving indigenous musical heritage)
- Mission-Texas.com (environmental justice)
- Publishing a book series through Xicana Chronicles.
- Preparing to launch my own line of musical and visual arts projects.
- Launching a Blog Talk Radio show via Xica Media on topics related to digital resistance.

How did your journey with digital resistance begin?

My journey through digital resistance was born out of blood and fire. It is inextricably linked to my personal, emotional, and spiritual journeys. The lessons I have learned have come out of daring to try unconventional ideas, making a ton of mistakes, and implementing visions that have come to me.

Initially, my digital warpath was carved from a place of anger and a culture of resistance. But as I grew, my digital work began to come from a place of creation and creativity. It no longer drew from a reactionary mindset, but one of asserting power, autonomy, creation, confidence, spirituality, and faith. Because resources were limited, I had to be rascuacha and put together all the free pieces to make a semi-functioning virtual machine. And it worked.

When I first became involved in the Mission community struggle in 2002, I had no understanding of organizing or utilizing technology for survival, healing, or liberation. It was through making mistakes and testing creative ideas that I began to understand the digital warpath. Even after thirteen years, I am still learning.

How was rascuacha tech born?

I come from the Westside of San Antonio, Texas and was born under white supremacy and segregation. Since I was little, I had been conscious of these things and how they made me feel as a young Xicanita. For example, my middle school was in the barrio and was predominantly Mexican American. However, its mascot was a Confederate soldier carrying the Confederate flag. Every time I got honor roll, I had a Confederate flag pinned to my lapel in a school ceremony. From the textbooks to the streets, white supremacy was reinforced in several spaces. It was a daily fact of life. My community's lands, history, culture, and tribal identity had been taken and there was a particular pain in my heart from this loss.

It was not until I got to the university that I found out that Mexican American Studies existed. My mind was blown. I began to understand myself and my historical context as a Xicana from Texas. I decided to make MAS my major because I felt a great thirst for more knowledge about my history. I quickly found out about MEChA (Movimiento Estudiantil Chicana/o de Aztlan) and became actively involved in justice campaigns on campus and off. It did not matter that I was a starving student, I learned there were all sorts of things I could do to help my community. I began working with Texas barrio communities on different campaigns and quickly noticed that across the board there were themes each struggle had in common. I also noticed that there existed pronounced technological divides.

In 2000, Creator introduced me to the Mission, Texas community and their ongoing struggles as survivors of cultural and environmental genocide. In the 1940s, the barrios of Mission became occupied by chemical corporations who established corporate pesticide production plants and railroad networks to and from the sites. It operated 24/7 for decades and was the birthplace of Agent Orange and many other concentrated and military-grade chemicals. For many years, it was the heart of the U.S. agrochemical (corporate farming pesticide) industry.

For over five decades the government, universities, and the chemical corporations used this community as a living experiment and observed the people as well as the local environment. They monitored disastrous levels of chemical contamination and cancer clusters while keeping the contamination hidden from the community. In 1980, the land was quietly classified as the #1 most contaminated site in the U.S. by the Environmental Protection Agency. It was later discovered that reports dating as far back as 1956 had documented health outbreaks around the facilities. In 1999, a class action lawsuit of over 3,000 affected community residents was filed against the 30 corporations that had run the operations in Mission.

In 2002, I heard about a reconvening of La Raza Unida political party from the Chicano Movement of the Civil Rights era. I got involved and began to learn more about the political process and community organizing at the statewide level. I ended up connecting with folks from across Texas who were interested in learning more about the Mission case. A few weeks later, a few of us went to Mission for a personal community tour.

At the time, I did not know how to build websites but I did know how to use a basic camera. So I ended up taking many pictures and recording heartbreaking stories shared by community members regarding the realities they faced due to the massive contamination and betrayal of the media and government. Taking pictures and recording short videos was the best I could do at the time. Even though I didn't know what to do next, I felt like it provided folks with an outlet to vent and release some of their suffering.

That visit changed my life. I felt like I had been to a war zone. A few days later, I began to feel like the footage we had taken was part of a previously secret history that needed to be shared publicly. I questioned the universe about what I was supposed to do with all the pictures and video footage. I didn't have money. I didn't have connections to the media. But I did have a laptop and some light tech skills. I went to the community and asked if they would be interested in building a website to share their stories and talk about the issue on their own terms.

And that is where rascuacha tech started for me. I realized that despite my own situations, my tech ability was a privilege that could possibly help. So I got online and started doing internet searches on how to build a website. This was in the era before blogging and Google, so I had to use Internet Explorer to search and often had to reword my questions to get the right answers. Eventually, I found the answers I was seeking and began to build a website one step and tutorial at a time. I didn't have any money to invest in any special features so I patched together as many free components as I could to bring the website to life. I wanted to doubt myself because I didn't have a degree and wasn't studying computers or a tech-related field. I eventually pushed myself past the doubt and began to produce the site.

The Mission-Texas.com website went live in 2005. After the release of the second version, which was in English and Spanish, I witnessed viewership skyrocket from 17 visitors a month to over 50,000 a month. This was a big deal, as it occurred before going viral was "a thing," in the land before Facebook and social media. Not much later, the class-action lawsuit settlement offers increased substantially. The EPA began to include the website and the community in meetings and processes as they conducted remediation. I realized that digital resistance represented a legitimate force and platform to stimulate direct action and positive change. I quickly began to see technology as a weapon of self-defense and a huge "f--- you" to white supremacy and "the system."

I also realized that I should not be ashamed for being rascuacha connecting all the digital pieces together in the most chafa way ever to make the virtual machine run. It did not matter that I didn't have the white man's pieces of paper to validate my tech abilities. I did the work I felt I was being called to do and that was enough for me.

How did you get into technology and multimedia?

Speak and Spell

Before I began public school, I spoke Spanish at home and knew very little English. One day, when I was about 5 years old, my parents brought home a little machine called the Speak and Spell by Texas Instruments. It was a thick, rectangular machine with a one-line screen display at the top, similar to that of a calculator, except that it displayed letters instead of numbers. It taught English pronunciation and spelling (in a terrible robotic voice) using different types of word and letter games.

I remember being very excited when my parents first brought it home. They told me it was expensive for them and that I needed to take really good care of it. I became glued to it and played with it every single day. I ended up learning how to spell and read in English in the year before I started school.

When I got to kindergarten, I was immediately tracked into the Gifted and Talented program because I was already reading, writing, and compiling stories with accompanying pictures. That same year I was asked by my kindergarten teacher to put together one of my "books" for a contest. I wrote, illustrated, and pasted together a small storybook about my first time meeting and interacting with the deer out in the Hill Country. As it turned out, that little book ended up being published in the school district anthology. I guess it could be said that I was officially published by the age of five.

It was not until I began writing <u>Rascuacha Tech</u> that I would remember this first book and understand that it was an early calling to my medicines. It was no coincidence that I was sharing stories using multimedia, which at that time (and at that age) was in written and art form. It was no coincidence that I was connecting with the deer, the animal relation directly tied to my sacred ancestral medicine. This event set the stage for visions of becoming an author one day, visions that would greet me again in my 30s.

Shortwave radio

I was born and raised in my mother's ancestral territory of Texas, but my father is from Cuba. He and my grandparents were guajiros (country folk) from Cuba who ended up in Texas after moving around Mexico and the U.S. due to the Cuban revolution and later, the Vietnam War. (My father was drafted to the Army after becoming a U.S. citizen and was eventually stationed in San Antonio.) Because of his own immigrant experience, my dad had an interest in connecting with (and always helping) people who did not speak English. One of his beloved possessions was an old shortwave radio that connected him to the world, a Zenith Transoceanic Royal D7000.

On some nights, he would tune into talk shows in different languages and on other nights we would catch baseball games, music, or dramas from Mexico. I remember hearing different music and stories from other places almost every night. I learned to appreciate connecting with other people and places through the shortwave radio. As a child, I fell in love with music, language, and the spoken word through the airwaves.

My first computer

I come from one of the first generations of public school kids that had computer classrooms. I remember we would play a game called Oregon Trail.

In that game, players would pretend to be white pioneers "settling" the Wild West. The object of the game was to survive the trail and try not to die from dysentery or an "Indian raid." Oregon Trail was the only thing I really knew about computers.

Then, one day (and out of the blue) my dad brings home a computer, the IBM PS/1. That day my world changed. The year was 1990 and I was 10 years old. The PS/1 could reach the internet through a connection called Prodigy. In those days, the internet streamed in colored, square pixels that would move and flash slowly (one pixel at a time) across the screen.

I used to think it was the coolest thing to go to Yahoo! to play board games online with random, unknown people across the world. It was a big deal back in my day. That computer took me from sitting in a makeshift office in a hot Texas car garage to the world. My understanding of my place in the world expanded.

Perhaps it is late by today's standards, but in 1990 at age 10, I began to communicate directly with people all over the planet. At the time, home computers and the internet were still relatively new to people. To write school reports my classmates and I would look up information in books and encyclopedias in public libraries. All schoolwork was written by hand. We listened to music on cassettes, but some people still had 8-track players. CDs had not yet arrived on the scene. Beepers had not hit the market yet, and it would be a few years before cell phones would become a phenomenon. We were at walkie-talkie technology and stylish (or not so stylish) landline telephones. We were barely crossing into "wireless" (landline) telephone technology. It was a different time. People still wrote letters and sent them by mail.

Not long after my dad brought home the computer, he brought home a dot-matrix printer. I started doing all my homework assignments on the computer just so that I could print them out. I incorporated printing into all sorts of class assignments, from basic everyday homework to reports...with custom painted covers and glitter. Yes, I was *that* kid.

I had a lot of fun as a student creating multimedia art to accompany my assignments. I began to participate in all the school contests I could. In middle school (1994) I even ended up winning second place in the Texas Media Awards, a statewide competition put together by the Texas Library Association. My life was definitely marked by the arrival of the home computer and the internet.

PREP

When I was in middle school, my mom found out about a program called PREP (Pre-Freshman Engineering Program) sponsored by the University of Texas in San Antonio. It was three summers long and taught low-income middle school students college-level math and engineering. I participated all three summers and excelled. It was through PREP that I learned about computer programming languages such as Basic. I also learned advanced logic, engineering, and physics. It gave me the opportunity to produce creative reports and projects with the computer. I eventually graduated at the end of those three years with honors and as one of the top three students with the highest grade point averages for the graduating class, citywide.

First job: legal secretary (age 12)

When I was 12 years old, I wanted to be a lawyer. I told my dad about it and that very weekend, he took me to meet a lawyer he knew. I remember being really excited about going to visit him at the Riverwalk and inside the historic Tower Life building with the gargoyles at the front door. We met with Mr. Price, who was very nice and who ended up hiring me to manage his office on the weekends. After some training from his main secretary, I was doing the job in no time. I ended up working for him every Saturday for the next three years. I learned how to answer phones, take messages, and (most importantly) maintain paper-based and computer-based filing systems. I became fascinated with the organization of data. The way information was stored in physical folders and on the computer resonated with my brain. This formed my foundation and love for archives and information architecture.

Has gender affected your work? How so?

Here are a few ways in which I believe gender has affected my work:

- Machismo and white supremacist patriarchy negatively affected my self-esteem and self-worth for many years.

- The journey to balance motherhood and activism taught me that I have a responsibility to care for myself. This has made me focus on exponentiality and making the most out of every action in the digital resistance war front.
- I have used my looks and gender to go undercover and access spaces of power.
- My struggles as a teen mom and womyn of color from Texas have heightened my sense of justice/injustice and made me more aware of systems of oppression.
- Home birth made me a better warrior because I learned to trust my body, intuition, and inner visions.

What forms of digital support are most requested by community movements?

The forms of digital support I have been approached about the most by community movements include:

- Digitizing documents and photos
- Designing event flyers
- Spreading the word online
- Designing logos
- Websites
- Setting up social media

In what ways has money affected the work?

Not having access to economic resources (personal/organizational/community) has been a huge obstacle. Despite the issues it has presented me (and community efforts) with, creativity has always found a way to burst forth. The pain of not having enough has also carved in me an unbreakable faith when it comes to overcoming obstacles. Not having money to do the work that needs to be done is what birthed rascuacha tech for me. It taught me that by taking small (but continuous) steps toward overcoming adversity, despair, and the feeling of powerlessness, that faith, strength, and resilience are forged.

CHAPTER 4: THE SPIRITUAL JOURNEY

Did your spiritual journey through ceremony affect your digital resistance work? How?

My journey through rascuacha tech and digital resistance happened in two parts: the projects before I began walking a path of ceremony and the projects after.

The spiritual and personal shifts I experienced as I began to decolonize affected my work. The spiritual path opened up to me midway through my digital journey and put me on a path of healing intergenerational and personal traumas.

Having been from the barrio and the segregated South, I had been keenly aware of white supremacy and machismo since I was very little. Years of aggressions had worn my spirit. For a long time, I walked with pain and anger for the things I had gone through. I reached a point where I didn't want to let my negative experiences hold me back anymore. I make a choice to heal so that I could keep growing and working toward the change I wanted to see in the world.

Eventually, the doorways of the Mexicayotl and ceremony opened for me through the Native American Church and danza. I went on a journey inward and experienced a paradigm shift. I began to understand the internet differently. I began to see positive and negative emotional reactions to web content. I saw how information affected individuals and groups in the physical world. I started to incorporate prayer into my work more often and noticed that placing positive intention and faith in my actions somehow made the work more powerful.

Case study: projects before ceremony

Mission-Texas.com (2005)

In 2005, I built a website to serve as the digital war front of the Mission Texas Coalition movement. It was a website that incorporated different types of information into a free digital library of news, upcoming events, secret legal hearing announcements, original blog posts, video, and other multimedia. The information was sorted chronologically and by media, type, and category. At the time it was built, CMS (content management systems) did not exist. I built it using Microsoft Publisher. I actually hand-designed two separate versions, which in today's terms would be the hand-built equivalent of using different themes in WordPress.

The color scheme of my first website was awful. I used a mix of loud, bright primary colors with no white background for text. It was built using Microsoft Publisher on a drag-and-drop system to draw and move boxes of text and designs. It was also multilingual...built manually by copying the horrible design from one page to another.

I spent way more time than I would like to remember constructing each these two versions. I made a lot of technical errors but eventually got the hang of it. I also got a lot of foundational knowledge out of creating a bilingual website by hand. I learned the hard way about the intricacies of a website.

I knew it was terrible, but I felt compelled to do something so I did the best I could with the resources I had at the time. Before this website went live, there was nothing about the Mission contamination or community resistance online. It had to start somewhere.

I spent way more time than I would like to remember constructing each these two versions. I also coded e-petitions where people from around the world would sign on to email blast local politicians and government offices. I imagine this does not sound like a big feat today, but at the time, it served as an effective fear tactic.

I made a lot of technical errors but eventually got the hang of it. I also got a lot of foundational knowledge out of creating a bilingual website by hand. I learned the hard way about the intricacies of a website before the blogging world appeared and changed the way a community-led movement could assert and grow digital autonomy.

When the site went live, it amplified and spurred life into the community resistance. The class-action lawsuit settlements increased from tens of thousands to five million. At the site's peak, we received over 50,000 visits a month...in the era before social networks. It forced the attorneys to be more open with their clients regarding upcoming hearing dates that would be leaked through the site. They had previously been accused of moving the case forward without consent from their clients on decisions.

We staged protests during hearings and special visits. We collectively documented everything as much as possible and shared it online. Eventually, our biggest "muscle" was promoting a documentary we had started producing using a very cheap camera that I would take with me to record community interviews and actions on-the-fly.

We began to have large community meetings and discuss multimedia strategies. We hosted events and invited local politicians to talk about the contamination. Community members began so speak publicly about the situation at numerous events and universities. When this issue connected with MEChA, it helped bring the case to UT Austin and the academic world. We connected with students from around the globe who were fighting contamination by the same corporations. The community's fight became intellectualized and a broader understanding of the issue came through identifying underlying historical and systemic conditions. And as understanding grew, public awareness, connection, interconnection, compassion, and action spread.

La Nueva Raza (2010)

La Nueva Raza news was a multilingual, multimedia community project I ran from 2004 to 2010. It consisted of a website, weekly e-newsletter, a weekday post, and a printed-paper that was distributed quarterly across the Southwest U.S. The idea to make a newspaper for the borderlands was born as a project out of the Raza Unida summits in Texas that began in 2002. I was a founding member of the project and collaborated closely with several Chicano activists primarily from Houston, Texas. Eventually (and due to my experience with the Mission Texas Coalition website), I took over the LNR website and print publications.

This project became my first passion project. It did not pay but it did consume a part of my daily life. The work and creative flow just poured out of me from a place deep within. My journey producing La Nueva Raza was intense on many levels. It taught me the value of hard work, of honoring the visions that came to me, of trust and community, of building virtually with others who I could and could not see...and of resistance. Through this project, I visited places like Washington D.C. and Boston to take part in radical media gatherings who were interested in our project.

One of the goals of LNR was to amplify the voices of the community at the center of the struggle. We wanted to encourage discussion, dialogue, and debate over the issues, events, politics, culture, and conditions relevant to Xicanxs. The news was not always happy, but the attempt was to move hearts and minds to action in the fight to obtain justice. It was not exactly reactionary, but it was based in a culture of resistance, which eventually wore on my soul.

When I began to build the LNR website for the first time, I decided I did not want to make the same mistakes I had made previously with the Mission-Texas.com website. I built it using a CMS platform (content management system) called Joomla! that was supposed to help manage large amounts of content. At the time, I was transitioning from hand-built websites on Microsoft Publisher to CMS. I realized after hand constructing the Mission-Texas.com site that I was producing more content than I could handle maintaining. Around the second year of my digital warpath, CMS came to the market and happened to address many of the issues I encountered in being able to manage large amounts of content easily and quickly.

It required some tech ability, but I trudged through it and built the first version of La Nueva Raza news in 2004 using that platform. It was through Joomla! that I learned how to access FTP and how to work with a theme template.

I was really intimidated to start jumping into codes and back-end things so I got online and looked up tutorials. If I typed a question and could not quickly find an answer, I rephrased my question until I found one. Through incessantly asking questions online, I found tons of information on how to do everything and anything I wanted. I just had to frame search online and take the time to read the documentation, taking each step slowly, one at a time.

After a few years of success and a steady following, I made a rookie mistake on the original La Nueva Raza site and lost the entire site and database. Because I was self-taught, I failed to follow one of the golden rules of managing a website: making a backup of the website and database. It was a horrible loss and for the rest of my life I will remember feeling that empty hole in my stomach when I realized that what I had just accidentally done could not be undone. I rebuilt the site as much as I could, using a new platform (at the time) called WordPress. I was able to rebuild it rather quickly, but it was not the same. Years of statistics, years of information was gone.

To this day, this second version of La Nueva Raza (built on WordPress) is still up and running even though the project no longer exists. This experience shook my foundation and made me feel that there had to be a better, less tech-heavy way to continue supporting my community. That is when I met WordPress. It was much easier than Joomla! and it introduced me to fusing websites with social media networks.

La Nueva Raza was a labor of love, but my heart felt called to do the work. Through LNR, I had the unique opportunity and responsibility of digitizing barrio community struggles that the media wouldn't talk about. But at the same time, this meant I was consuming a lot of pain and suffering. At times, it made me feel like I lived in a hopeless world.

Case study: projects after ceremony

After years of working on the Mission case and La Nueva Raza, I felt very spiritually heavy. The pain I was witnessing filled me with a deep sense of injustice and bitterness. The world I was seeing was violent and filled with darkness. Although I saw resistance as a ray of light, its premise was reactionary, requiring the injustice in order to exist.

In my early 20s, I felt a calling inside my heart to heal, reconnect with Spirit, and begin to live in a way that could honor earth and life. I did not want to see the suffering anymore. I wanted to communicate with nature again. I wanted to return to the things I knew before "Jesus" and "the devil" had been put into my consciousness.

After many years, the doorways began to open all at once. First, the temazcal appeared. Then came the danza, followed by the tipi. I interpreted these things as signs from the universe that my prayers were being answered. I was ready to make the journey inward.

The first time I sat before the fire in tipi, the very first thing I felt in my heart was an overwhelming feeling of having come back home after a long time of being away. When I went to my first temazcal and had to throw myself on the wet dirt because the steam was so hot, I felt the earth hug me and pull me back in time. When I did my first danza in the Arizona desert and felt a rush move through me and shoot up and out through my head as I danced, I knew I was connected to all creation, and that my entire life and all my hardships had happened for a reason.

After finding the medicine, I thought about justice differently. I realized that we should not be asking for power, that we should be asserting the power we already had. I also felt there was something to be said about a culture of resistance versus a culture of autonomy, compassion, life, and creation.

I continued to work on La Nueva Raza but the work definitely slowed. I was at a crossroads with regard to how I lived my life and what my purpose really was through this work. This process of slowing the activism and shifting into a spiritual path lasted about two years and saw me through a huge personal shift that nearly broke my spirit. At the end of that journey, the last piece I did for La Nueva Raza led me directly to meet Huehuetl and Yetlanezi. I did not know it at the time, but this also set the stage for my own journey into music.

Xica Media (2012)

Xica Media was originally born as an attempt to financially free myself from working for the man and the system. Two years after my last La Nueva Raza post, I was working in a high-level state government position and stressed out of my mind. The daily micro and macro aggressions were making my spirit sick. I recognized this, yet I had no other option but to keep working there. The economy was bad and this job was keeping my family financially afloat. I went to ceremony a lot but found it difficult to come back to work Monday morning to be surrounded by hate...for a paycheck.

Up until this point in my life, I had built a negative relationship with money. I had begun to see it as the root of evil, exploitation, and injustice. But with two children and another on the way, it was no longer possible to stretch myself so thin. I decided to give myself a chance and try to market myself as a multimedia professional to help support my family.

At first, I had two major struggles: 1. valuing and respecting the value of my own work to quote a fair price that respected my ability and time, and 2. getting over my guilt of charging people and projects for my services.

I went a good two years trying to reconcile these things but finally reached a tipping point after moving to Mexico. Everything changed when I was forced to become part of the virtual workforce. I learned that my skills had value.

At first, I repeated the old pattern of taking odd internet jobs and doing community work on the side. As I continued participating in the virtual workforce, I began to learn the going prices for each of my skills...and that they, along with my command of U.S. English, had a real competitive advantage and monetary value. I ended up moving away from the idea of Xica Media and embracing my professional, individual self as a "freelancer."

By 2015, I was driving internet traffic through the different channels more than I was making dollars. I decided to let go of Xica Media as an income stream and launch

XicaMedia.com as an umbrella page for the digital resistance networks. Although I do not blog on Xica Media just yet, my hope is that this book will lay the groundwork for more active participation and communication through that site around the topics of digital resistance and rascuacha tech.

Huehuetl (2012)

Huehuetl was an intergenerational musical family ensemble from Jalisco who specialized in preserving indigenous Mexican music and instrumentation. Huehuetl was composed of a father, mother, and their three adult children. The group had started in the 1970s and was in its fourth decade.

It was my first time working with an effort that was not focused around a community struggle, but instead on preserving culture. It represented a radical departure for me in terms of my digital warrior path. It wasn't resistance in the way I had known it. It resonated with me because I began to see the importance of digitally preserving culture and music. It represented the beginning of a new, yet related path of digitization, decolonization, and curación for my work.

I built the site using WordPress but was not happy with the theme. I used this opportunity to learn more about CSS (cascading style sheets) because I wanted to incorporate vivid imagery of ancient Mexico into the site. Because I had never worked on anything that required as strong of a visual aesthetic, it took some time for my work to become artistic.

Yetlanezi (2012)

Yetlanezi was an offshoot of Huehuetl, composed of the 2nd generation of the Borsegui family. This project departed from the strictly instrumental sound of Huehuetl and blended the ancient instrumentation with electronica.

I built the Yetlanezi website using Wordpress and soon became responsible for the English content. In the beginning, it was hard for me to describe their music in a non-academic or non-spiritual way. I had been to shows where their music called the wind, causing it to swirl around the audience, leaving them somewhere in between frightened and enchanted. I struggled with several versions of the site but did eventually find balance in language that honored the spiritual elements with the professional.

Over the years, I took on many backstage and production roles. I learned a great deal about management, production, marketing, and graphic design. I helped produced the first official Yetlanezi CD 100% in-house. This process boosted confidence in my rascuacha tech abilities and led to the founding of Tezcatlipoca Records.

Tezcatlipoca Records (2013)

After a few years of working with Yetlanezi, my collaboration with the group could no longer be defined as strictly "Yetlanezi" because the work had begun to bridge with the activist and rascuacha tech roots of Xica Media. Thus, Tezcatlipoca Records was born. It became our musical "publishing house" and label through which the Yetlanezi CDs (and one day, my own musical project) would be produced. In establishing this as a production house, we also opened the door to help others who were producing indigenous-themed music.

The birth of this site was revolutionary for me. It represented a coming-of-age event as it crossed me over from being a digital warrior to a musical artist.

The one-page site was built on WordPress using a default theme and header image I created. It is by far the easiest website I have ever built.

Xica Nation (2014)

Xica Nation was born out of a vision that came to me when I first moved to Guadalajara in 2013. Having grown up in Texas, I knew a lot of things about northern Mexican culture. But central Mexico was a bit different from what I knew. Interestingly, one of the things that helped me adjust the most was having gone to ceremony.

It was through my identity as a native person that I came to feel more at home in Jalisco. From foods to daily practices to street names, Nahuatl language remains very much alive and part of the local dialect. Huichol culture is also very present. I had experienced both back home in ceremony, which led me to realize that I was connected to the culture in Jalisco. It served as a reminder that I, as a Xicana and Tejana, was connected to the continent in a present and living (not just historical) way. I felt a need to share this with my Xicanx nation relatives in the U.S. who were also on a journey to decolonize...but how?

One day a vision came to me: to create a virtual community library where our indigenous culture as Xicanxs could be collected and shared. It would be used to help people step outside of the false and divisive labels such as "Latino" and "Hispanic." I wanted to create a space to be inclusive of tribal life ways as well as detribalized peoples who were on a journey to decolonize.

I quickly reserved XicaNation.com but sat with it for almost an entire year before the vision of the site design came to me. I prayed for the universe to guide me and once the vision came, I worked day and night to manifest what I was seeing in my mind. I made many mistakes along the way, especially since the blogging world had changed so much since my time in La Nueva Raza. But the site immediately went viral and to date continues to be a fountain of indigenous identity-affirming information. The site has a wealth of information that includes music, links to codices, and other sources of ancestral knowledge. More recently, I have begun to interview community leaders as well as write original articles related to our modern day experiences of decolonization.

Xicana Chronicles (2014)

The Xicana Chronicles project was born out of a need to vent and express myself as a radical Xicana on a journey to decolonize. After years of promoting the voices of others and simultaneously dealing with my own difficult personal situations, I felt a need to carve a creative space for myself to blossom and vent artistically. I offered the floor to other mujeres, specifically rowdy Tejana artivists, to share their arts so that we could have a safe communal space to document and publish our experiences. The Dedication page reads:

Xicana Chronicles is the living diary of the 21st century Xicana. It seeks to document, preserve, and amplify the Xicana experience in the words and arts of womyn warriors and mujeres xingonas.

It aims to serve as a herstorical collection of multimedia first-hand accounts of this generation and time. This space represents an act of resistance and resilience and is dedicated to encouraging Xicanas to write, publish, share, and create our own herstories.

This is a modern-day codex that documents the landscape and intricacies of life as Xicana womyn. It documents numerous intersections of daily life, love, self-love, family, spirituality, culture, consciousness, and decolonization as experienced by self-identified Xicanas in their personal lives, homes, workplaces, societies, and political regimes.

I was living in Guadalajara when I launched this project, which took place just a few months after the successful launch of Xica Nation, and one year after having left my territory (Texas) and never having returned. I envisioned a radical space where other mujeres would actively contribute content. I defined "success" as the site and/or posts going viral. I also wanted to crossover into art and branch out from being a "tech." I figured that at the very least and if no one cared, I would have a cool space to share my art and writing. There was no room in my vision for "failure."

Since its launch in July of 2014, Xicana Chronicles has amassed a cult following from individuals, groups, and universities around the world. Six months later, I felt my first moment of success when I reached 1,000 shares on a controversial post within 24 hours. It has grown by leaps and bounds and includes a growing array of original pieces by contemporary indigenous Xicana Tejana artists and writers.

One year into the project, I felt a calling to turn Xicana Chronicles a publishing house and publish four books, representing my prayers to the four directions. This text is the first book and will hopefully lay the groundwork for the success of the following books.

End Family Detention (2014)

The End Family Detention website was built in 2014 and represented a return to grassroots activism and community resistance for me. It was built as an emergency response to the family detention crisis in the U.S. In the summer of 2014, thousands of mothers and unaccompanied children who were fleeing war and violence in Central America arrived at the U.S. border seeking asylum. They began to be kidnapped by the U.S. government and enslaved in private for-profit "family" prisons in remote areas of the country. Many of them were of Mayan descent and did not speak English or Spanish.

I was approached by a friend and respected human rights activist lawyer, Virginia Raymond, to become part of a grassroots network of activists that formed as an emergency response to this crisis. Letters by the imprisoned mothers and children had been written and smuggled out, eventually getting to me out of desperation. Because I was in Mexico, I could only do so much...so I contributed by building the EndFamilyDetention.com website with the intention to support this network of activists while serving as a free, public, living, digital archive of the crisis.

Eventually and with many prayers and the invaluable, incessant efforts of radical womyn warriors on the ground, the website came to life and the digitized letters of the mothers and children quickly went viral. Thanks to the efforts of Virginia Raymond (who was instrumental in reaching out to the academic and linguistic communities) professional translations started to pour in and letters began being read around the world. It became statistically evident that the voices of the moms and kids were being heard and shared across social media in multiple languages.

We eventually connected with students in Guatemala (again, thanks to Virginia Raymond) and we ended up making internet history by collaborating with them to make EndFamilyDetention.com a tri-lingual resistance site in two European (English, Spanish) and one previously undigitized, unwritten Mayan language - Tz'utujil.

A year into the digital resistance, CultureStrike, a radical arts organization out of California, approached us one day about the Visions From The Inside project where 15 artists from across the U.S. teamed up to create an art piece out of the letters. This particular project went viral and garnered more media attention that we ever imagined. It eventually went on display at the United Nations Palais des Nations in Geneva for one week during the Human Rights council sessions on child migrants.

From the start of my participation in End Family Detention to the present, I have prayed incessantly for visions, insight, and protection. The first month I created the site I fell into a depression because I was simply in shock and disbelief at what was happening. But as we launched campaigns in solidarity with actions led by the mothers and children inside the prisons, public awareness grew and some of them were able to win their cases. As the site went viral time after time, effort after effort, with one crazy idea after another, it was statistically clear that we had created a successful space that fostered awareness, direct action, and healing. And while I still feel the sadness of the situation as I continue to contribute to that effort, I have learned not to let it consume me.

CHAPTER 5: SPIRITUAL ELEMENTS OF THE VIRTUAL WORLD

The following is based solely on my opinion and individual experience.

Is there a spiritual component to digital resistance?

The digital warfront is a sacred space. It is the virtual (and global) fireplace for the movement. A digital warrior is the keeper of the virtual fire. As the fire grows, so does the exposure, energy, and momentum of the movement on the ground and across the globe.

There exists a direct link between the physical, spiritual, and digital worlds. All three worlds deal with forces unseen that can affect one's state of mind, emotions, physical reactions, and spirit. I believe that in the virtual world, spiritual attacks move through the consumption of digitized content that stimulate hate, ignorance, insensitivity, fear, and suffering. They are highly contagious and can immediately manifest in the physical world. A digital warrior must remain vigilant of the spiritual forces at play that evoke different sentiments on the ground and online.

I see negative imagery and news as spiritual warfare. Lately, I've been seeing media coverage of political events that I would also label as spiritual warfare. Colonialism and white supremacy are projected, protected, and reinforced through corporate multimedia. Despite or because of these things, we should be proactive about tending to our inner light. We should disconnect for a little bit. We should seek positive information to lift our spirits. Because dealing with spiritually heavy information is required for a digital resistance warfront, a digital warrior must consciously (and routinely) consume positive information. I learned this lesson the hard way through La Nueva Raza, the Mission Texas Coalition, and End Family Detention.

What are the top three spiritual concepts you have come across the most in your digital works?

1. The way of the death eaters (physical/psychological/spiritual cannibalism and biocide)
2. Fear
3. Starting and spreading of dark digital fires

What is the "way of the death eaters" and how does it relate to digital resistance?

I am still exploring different terms to describe this concept, but I felt the need to discuss it in this text at this time. What I call the **"way of the death eaters"** is a highly infectious psychosis that economically, physically, psychologically, and spiritually feeds on death and suffering in increasing magnitudes. It can spread from person to person via the physical, spiritual, and virtual worlds. It is not a way of life, it is a way of death. It is a conscious and unconscious death cult that people knowingly and unknowingly participate in. It is genocidal, ecocidal, suicidal, and cannibalistic in nature. Its symptoms include apathy, ignorance, insensitivity, and a host of other ills that dehumanize and destroy.

There are two other words that very closely describe what I see moving through the internet. The first word to describe the philosophy behind what I witnessed is "wétiko." As described in Columbus and Other Cannibals by Jack D. Forbes, wétiko is a word from the Cree nation meaning "cannibal" that refers to an extremely contagious mental sickness where humans feed on the death and suffering of other humans for profit.

Before coming across Forbes' book, I had referred to the social, political, systemic consumption of humans and nature for profit as the "way of the death eaters" and the "wasi'chu path." The word "wasi'chu is Lakota and translates into "takers of the fat." It can be derogatory. For me, that word also emphasizes the human path one should not walk in relation to the earth and all creation.

Perhaps the terms I use will change in the future. At the moment, all these words describe the same thing I am seeing moving across the virtual world. Their manifestation across that medium should not be taken lightly, because as they spread online, they manifest in the physical world.

This is another reason why digital resistance cannot simply consist of negative information or multimedia. The same way these ills can spread online, so can hope, light, encouragement, community, growth, and healing.

How does fear relate to digital resistance?

I believe that fear can move through the virtual world and manifest physically. Online it moves through digital fires in the form of corporate media propaganda, hate speech, threats, trolling, or cyber bullying.

Protecting one's spirit is part of the digital warpath. Regardless of whether fear moves through multimedia or the physical world, the same curación, remedios, and protección can still be used. At the end of the day, you are still communicating with people. The virtual world is simply the vehicle.

What is a "digital fire" and how can it be a form of spiritual warfare?

Digital fires occur when an individual has an emotional response to web-based information. In that moment of interconnection, a "fire" is metaphorically lit in someone's heart. It can be light and foster compassion and interconnection. It can be dark and evoke negative emotions. Examples of this include (but are not limited to) cyberbullying, trolling, hate speech, or biased corporate media perspectives on an issue.

Within the realm of digital resistance, negative responses to the community resistance should never be internalized or taken personally. Meeting those responses with emotion is draining to the mind and spirit. That energy can be used to do something more productive. From a strategical perspective (and statistically speaking) any reference to the movement online, whether it is positive or negative, creates an avenue of web traffic in its direction and increases search engine visibility. Even if subjected to a dark digital fire, one does not have to permit a digital fire to burn them.

How can a digital warrior protect their spirit?

I do not believe that a particular belief system or religion is the best way to protect one's spirit. I can only speak to my experience, which has been in two parts: the time before I stepped into tipi and the Mexicayotl and the time after.

I incorporate several practices into my daily work routines. I pray daily about the work I am being called to do. I try to be conscious about limiting the amount of negative information I consume online because I feel that it can negatively impact my spirit and dissipate my faith. When dealing with topics of human suffering, I try to balance the ugly truths with information that stimulates action and hope.

The Mexicayotl and ceremony paths are teaching me about being in equilibrium with all creation. I believe these same teachings apply to the physical, spiritual, and virtual worlds.

In what ways has your own personal process of decolonization affected your work?

While my own personal decolonization process has been painful, it has also gifted me a multidimensional vision that continues to help me navigate physical, virtual, and spiritual landscapes. It has made me realize the connection between all my experiences, the historical context I was born into, and my present sociopolitical context. Having an understanding of where I come from, who I am, and where I am empowers me and my digital work greatly. The mere fact that I, a Xicana woman with indigenous roots to this continent, continue to exist is a form of resistance. I come from a line of warriors who have survived centuries of genocide. I am the answered prayers of my ancestors and I feel deeply moved to be taught their life ways as I move through the virtual world.

Decolonizing has helped me better understand the way spiritual energies move across the virtual realm. Decolonizing has also allowed me to have a deeper understanding of the importance of my own digital footsteps. For generations, our history and sacred knowledge has been burned and banned. I now understand that the contributions of digital warriors construct a virtual codex that can never be burned. I have also learned that inserting Spanish or Nahuatl words into English-dominant websites serve to decolonize the internet and the English lexicon.

Decolonizing has brought me to question practicing a culture of resistance versus one of creation. It is not just about reacting to the negative things that happen to our communities. We should not define and limit ourselves to exist only when oppression exists. As part of a digital generation, digital resistance warriors have a responsibility to hold down the virtual front lines and to digitize our experiences so that our cultures can be retained, expressed, and shared across the planet, regardless of whether we remain under attack.

What are the top five mistakes to avoid within the spiritual realm of digital resistance?

1. Not engaging in a daily spiritual practice.
2. Not protecting your mind from the way of the death eaters/the wasi'chu path/wétiko.
3. Listening to or spreading fear.
4. Not establishing equilibrium in the amount of positive and negative information you consume through multimedia.
5. Spreading negative emotion and not evoking a sense of responsibility, hope, or direct action on the matter at hand.

PART III: INSIDE THE MACHINE

CHAPTER 6: HOW TO CONSTRUCT A DIGITAL WAR FRONT

I am humbled at the power we as a digitized generation have at our fingertips. We have the power to preserve and create our own codices digitally and communally. We can create and share our stories directly with the world and in real-time. However, in communities of color that are under attack, resources are increasingly limited. These communities face ongoing trauma, lack of economic resources, media blackout, backlash from the non-profit industrial complex, technological divides, and communication barriers. Constructing a virtual identity can help combat these ills and support the community-led movement. This is where rascuacha tech comes into play.

In the next few pages, you will find resource-friendly techniques to construct digital resistance movements that document, digitize, and disseminate information to boost online visibility, raise awareness, grow action-oriented networks, and assert digital power. You will learn the basics of how to create a digital war front that serves as a multimedia, multilingual platform with the power to disseminate in real-time, automatically, and globally.

Stories of my personal experiences are sprinkled throughout the following sections and are intended to serve as lessons learned.

There are different types of websites and there are many ways to build a web presence. You have to think critically about the type of digital space that works best for the community's goals and available resources. If you are looking to build user engagement and want to expand your virtual audience, preliminary planning needs to take place. If you seek to create a static website that points to a social media page (where the bulk of communication exchange takes place) careful planning is still required.

Things to consider with respect to the design and functionality of a website include:

- Digital volunteers
- Available resources
- An understanding of the likes, dislikes, and patterns of your intended audience

- An understanding of the likes, dislikes, and patterns of the audience of the opposition
- A critical analysis of the methods/patterns of offense on behalf of the opposition
- An understanding of what the internet is saying/not saying about your struggle
- Constant observation, critical analysis, and rollout of measurable improvements and user experiences

The goals of the digital war front must be established by the community at the center of the struggle. However, digital warriors have a responsibility to make their community aware that their input is critical to planning a successful online campaign strategy. In terms of usability, getting feedback from trusted friends, family, or even strangers - regardless of their tech ability - can provide insight and spur creativity and innovation.

What I offer in this text is a basic framework that can be modified to fit the circumstances of the movement you are involved in. You do not need to be an expert to build a website. Just do the best you can with what you have.

What are the components of a well-rounded virtual identity?

By using some of the methods I will outline shortly, the movement can save time, energy, and money. My methods are not the only way to demand justice or digitally resist. Some methods may or may not work perfectly for your particular situation. As I mentioned in the beginning, my goal is not to create a one-size-fits-all strategy. The intention is to level the playing field by outlining basic standards of technological knowledge for supporting movements led by communities of color. These methods were developed with the understanding that the power and the platform belong to the community.

Constructing a website is very much like building a house. There are different parts of a home to consider, including the land, foundation, blueprint, frame, style, functionality, colors, material, etc. The same concepts apply to constructing a virtual space.

The following are free/low-cost components that can be used together to construct a website and digital war front:

- Domain name
- Hosting (web space)
- Platform
- Social media networks
- Multimedia networks

Domain name

The domain name is the word or words that are typed into the address bar at the top of your browser. It is what appears after the http://www. such as http://www.<u>fill-in-the-blank.com</u>. It is similar to the street address of a house.

Domains can be used if you purchase your own hosting or if you use a free service to run the site. Once it is purchased, it is "pointed" to a specific folder or address. It can be purchased online through many providers. I will warn you now that when deciding on which company to use, a cheaper price does not equate to a better deal. Sometimes receiving quality customer service in times when you need urgent technical assistance can be priceless.

I have paid anywhere from $2 to 16 dollars for a year for a domain via Go Daddy. For an additional cost, what is known as "privacy" can be purchased. By law, the owner of a domain name must be publicly listed. By purchasing privacy, the name of the hosting company appears in place of the name of the individual owner.

Planning your domain name is of critical importance because it defines who you are and what you do. If it is poorly planned or too long, it can discourage audiences from finding you. There are a million names to choose from, but you have to do your research. Check the names you are interested in using to see if they are available. Also, search for the names that are being used for related efforts. If the name you were searching for is already taken, investigate to see what its purpose is and check the .com and .org versions to see what is available. Nowadays you can find domain names that have a .com or a .org "extension" (the final part of your website's name.) If ABC.com is taken, you could potentially purchase ABC.org or ABC.us or any other available extension, so that you get to keep the name you want. The most common form is .com for a domain name but that is quickly changing and now there are different extensions such as .info or others that are based on specific genres and industries. Because I am a Go Daddy customer, I use Go Daddy to research domain names to find out what is and is not available.

Hosting (web space)

Hosting is the virtual space that the website will be built on. It can be compared to an empty lot where a house is to be constructed.

Hosting must be purchased and costs around $130 a year (up front) to $16.00 a month. Personally, I have remained a loyal customer to my hosting provider (GoDaddy.com) for many years because of their excellent customer service. I know they may not be the least expensive option, but when tech emergencies strike, their assistance has proven to be invaluable.

It is not required for the domain and the hosting to be purchased from the same company. However, it does make things easier for the person creating the website to connect the domain to the hosting when that is the case.

Platform

The platform of a website is similar to the frame of a house. To build a site that needs to manage and display a lot of data, I recommend using a CMS framework such as WordPress or Joomla!. I have found much success in using WordPress and complementing it with automated social media posting on Facebook, Twitter, and Google+.

Creating a website for a movement is a great way to archive information and curate it publicly. While social media offers interaction and engagement, it does not offer easy ways to store documents and curate information. That is not its purpose.

I strongly suggest that beginners research the latest trends and pick a CMS platform that works best for them. For the purposes of this text, I will be discussing the WordPress framework.

Social media networks

Social media networks as automated, secondhand publishing houses. While some social media experts recommend shaping community or business social media accounts into actively-engaged virtual personalities, that requires the resource of time. Using social media as an automated secondhand publishing house has been successful for my efforts and has generated more web traffic than I could have ever imagined.

Utilize the social media networks that work best for you and your situation. If you choose to create a static website and use social media as your primary avenue for communication, time and person power is a resource that will need to be considered. If you choose to use social media as a secondary publishing house, time and effort are still required, but they can be minimized. My personal recommendation is to do the best that you can with what you have at the moment.

Multimedia networks

You can use multimedia networks to produce content in a particular format that can be imported into your WordPress site and then disseminated via your social media accounts. There are free and paid (premium) ways to make this happen. Multimedia networks such as YouTube and Blog Talk Radio offer free ways to produce video and audio. Shows or episodes published through those streams can later be embedded and archived in the main website.

What are the costs involved?

Hosting plans can be purchased and paid for by the year or month. I have paid anywhere from $130 a year to $16 a month for an unlimited hosting plan.

I have paid anywhere from $1 to $16 for a domain name for one year. Go Daddy offers frequent discounts for new domains and hosting plans, so I have often taken advantage of this and gotten domain names for really cheap for the first year. Domain names must be renewed every year and can have an added layer of privacy.

By law, the owner of the domain name must be listed publicly. For an extra charge you can purchase what is known as "privacy" and have the owner listed as the domain name company you use (instead of you.) The charge for privacy is in addition to the cost of the domain. Privacy costs something around the range of $16-$25 per domain, per year.

How can you purchase a domain name and hosting plan?

There are two ways to manage the web space that will be used for constructing a digital warfront. If there are no funds to secure the cost of hosting and maintaining your own core files, WordPress offers a free, but limited version that allows content to be published and shared. This version does not allow much control over the design and functionality of the website.

If funds can be secured to pay for hosting, the full version of WordPress can be installed on the hosting plan. Advanced users will be able to access core files via the Editor or FTP to edit the design and functionality. You can search online for a "hosting provider" and purchase the plan instantly. There are hosting providers that offer yearly and monthly payment plans.

Regardless of whether you purchase a hosting plan or not, you have the option to purchase a domain name, which would give the virtual space you will be occupying its own custom address. You can purchase it from your hosting provider or any other company. Once purchased, the domain name needs to be "directed" to the "root" or webpage that will serve as the homepage for the website.

When it comes to domains and hosting, keep in mind that cheaper is not always better. I am a long time Go Daddy customer so I purchase both the domain name and hosting from them and easily connect one to the other. Using Go Daddy has not been the least expensive option, but I have found their products very easy and quick to connect.

Why WordPress?

I began working with WordPress after working with Microsoft Publisher and Joomla!. I started out hand-designing websites from scratch using a drag-and-drop design system, then I transitioned to coding PHP and CSS using Joomla!, not knowing what I was doing and making a ton of mistakes. At first, I thought Joomla! was pretty cool. It was super complicated at points, but okay once I figured out the code to make the site look the way I wanted. However, when I came across WordPress (which was free at that time) I realized that a lot of the extra work I was manually doing could be automated. The coding was still necessary, but I did not need to mess too much with it because I found templates and plugins I liked on WordPress. I also really appreciated the way WordPress allowed for new posts to be automatically shared via email and across social media at once, a feature that I had invested a very significant amount of time in doing manually in the past. I used to do one round of copying and pasting links into emails, another round of copying and pasting into a Google group, followed by another round of the same written and coded for the social media of the era (MySpace.) It was a difficult and painstaking labor of love that required a ridiculous amount of time. With WordPress, I was able to cut the amount of time I needed to invest dissemination and design, which then allowed me to focus on content.

One other important reason that I continue to choose WordPress is because of its learning curve, which is not that steep. I am able to work with larger groups of people who may not be that technologically savvy but who can access the millions of free training resources online on how to use WordPress. So I find it very easy to collaborate with others using this platform.

What are posts, hashtags, social media, and multimedia?

Posts, hashtags, social media, and multimedia represent different ways to document, digitize, and disseminate our stories. Within the realm of digital resistance, these represent digital bits of information that we can use (mostly for free) to add our voices to the virtual world. They are public, permanent, and automatically receive a digital timestamp and have a global reach. These are the arrows of the digital warrior.

Posts and pages are parts of the WordPress blogging platform. A **post** is a piece of content that belongs to a collection of information on a particular topic. It is information shared with time and date in mind. For example, publishing information on a weekly basis would be done via a post. A **page** contains static content on a website. Such informational pages include the "About Us" or "Contact Us" pages.

A **hashtag** is a word or phrase (written with no space) that is preceded by the hashtag symbol, such as #ILoveCoffee. Hashtags can be added to posts or pages but are intended to create spaces for public discussion via social media.

Through hashtagging, a conversation with a particular hashtag becomes curated on each social media platform it appears within. For example, if you type #ILoveCoffee into a Facebook post, you are creating a conversation that can be viewed by the entire Facebook user base. Others can chime into the conversation by using the same hashtag. If you make a similar post on Twitter with the same #, you create that conversation within Twitter and make it viewable to the Twitter public.

This can be a useful strategy when creating a campaign that requires direct public action. Catchy, creative hashtag phrases for movements or particular campaigns can help increase the chances of virality.

Social media comes in different forms known as "platforms" and is intended for people around the world to connect with their friends, family, and other personal networks. Facebook is one form of social media and Twitter is another. Different "social media platforms" offer different advantages. In Facebook, you can share images or text. In Twitter, you can share short statements of 120 characters or less. On other social media platforms like Pinterest, you can share images. You may find that using one social media platform is easier than using another and that is perfectly fine.

It is good to engage with your social media audience, make friends, and contribute to group conversations. Sharing is caring in the virtual world. The more the digital war front can connect with people, the more likely the content will be shared across the digital world. However, if time and person power are not available resources, social media engagement must be gauged. At a minimum, it should include post sent via automated publishing from the WordPress site.

Multimedia is content in different forms - audio, visual, or text-based.

NOTE: Multimedia networks are defined here.

Content can be created in many different forms. To increase user engagement with the piece (which increases the likelihood that the user will share the information with their networks) you should always assign a featured image to a post, weave images and links throughout the text, and/or include embedded video/audio from other multimedia networks, if you have them.

A digital resistance war front is more than just a website. It stimulates senses and emotions and affects real people. Through utilizing different forms of multimedia, a digital resistance war front has the power to reach across any computer screen in the world and make a real human connection in real-time.

How to construct a website using WordPress

Once the hosting plan has been purchased, the host will provide you with login credentials to access your account. You will need to log into your account and locate the option to install an "app" or application. Look for the WordPress application and begin the installation process. Depending on your provider, you may need to look around the site to locate the option to install.

Most hosting companies offer an easy, one-click installation for WordPress. However, if you encounter any issues or need additional help, you should contact your hosting company for specific instructions on how to install WordPress using their site.

During the process of installing WordPress, you will be asked to create a username and password for the new site as well as for the database, which contains and curates all the data of a website. Accessing a database directly requires special software as well as some knowledge of SQL (structured query language.) Because my knowledge is limited in this area, I do not usually dabble in the database. However, one thing I have learned the hard way is that the database should be backed up frequently. I explain ways to back up the site in further detail on the section covering Backups.

Once WordPress has been successfully installed, you should receive the login credentials via e-mail for the new site.

Log into WordPress using the credentials. You will arrive at what is called the "dashboard." It is the main administration page in the back-end of a website. From the dashboard, posts and pages can be managed, image libraries can be maintained, users can be added or removed, and other general customizations can be made.

At this point, the website has been created. Think of it as a newly-built house whose frame and walls have been set up. However, they still need to be painted and other parts of the home still need to be added.

There are a million ways to modify your WordPress installation. Luckily, a simple internet search can lead you to great written and video tutorials that can help guide you as you begin to develop the website.

At this point, we are going to take a pause on the site construction and take a moment to relook at our plan so that we can take note of all the things that need to be developed. As we build, we need to make sure the digital resistance war front is as well-constructed as possible.

Designing the front end

In the first moments that a user lands on your site, emotion is evoked through the images, fonts, colors, content, level of language used and usability. The top part of a website that first appears when someone lands on the site is referred to as the section "above the fold." It should display all pertinent links and information so that the site visitor does not have to scroll down. The website has a few moments to draw the attention of the site visitor and encourage them to read more and click on links within the site.

Planning around your intended audience is critical. Never assume that the site you have built is as user-friendly for everyone else as it is for you. As it is being built, ask others to visit the site and give you constructive feedback. In this process, ego has to be set aside in order to grow. A smooth-running virtual war front is built with time and lots of trial and error. Being humble will help you through this process.

Here are some recommended components that I believe are critical to a digital resistance war front:

- Relevant and eye-catching imagery
- Multimedia
- Interactive spaces to engage
- Contact us
- About us
- News section
- Events section

Relevant and eye-catching imagery

It is critical to use appropriate colors and relevant imagery to keep site visitors engaged. A catchy, graphic logo is important but not necessary, as standard text can be used to display the title of a site. When creating posts and pages, always attach featured images before publishing. Featured images appear across social media and wherever the "feed" (published content listing) is displayed, including on the front page of your WordPress site. The more relevant and attractive an image is, the higher likelihood that someone who stumbles across your link will click on it to learn more.

Multimedia

By creating content using different multimedia, you increase your chance for exponentiality and reaching a greater audience. For example, if you have a site that contains great images plus some YouTube hosted videos, you are able to reach folks that prefer not to read. If you produce audio content, you could reach an audience that listens to online radio who might not be into videos or social media. Inserting downloadable PDF files will reach users who seek in-depth information about the case. People obtain and perceive information differently, so the more multimedia is incorporated, the broader the audience that can be reached.

Interactive spaces to engage

Creating interactive spaces for visitors to engage with you on a site requires the right theme options or "plugins" in order to support that functionality. Relationships with your audience are strengthened when you create opportunities to interact using images, video, audio or clickable options that allow the user to engage with the site. Crafting an easy and positive user experience increases the likelihood that the site visitor shares your site, post, or page.

Contact us

It is always important to let the media and public know how to contact the movement. You should create a page (not a post) to publish this information. The Contact Us page could contain a "form" where basic information is collected and sent to a private email address and email administrator. I suggest inserting a form into the Contact Us page versus displaying an email address because it increases the likelihood of spam.

Also, a link to reach the Contact Us page should be clearly displayed in the main menu as well as in the footer section.

About us

To establish a sense of trust and relationship, it is critical to define what the purpose of the website is and who the force is behind the content or production. A website administrator does not always need to be listed, nor do real and individual names need to be revealed. Defer to the community about what this page needs to say and always put safety first.

News section

By assigning a News category for posts, they can be displayed in a number of ways which will evoke a sense of movement and action around the movement. A chronological list of posts can be easily displayed on a dedicated News page or on the front-page. Whether there is actual momentum around the movement on the ground or not, the digital resistance war front needs to evoke a sense of ongoing activity, which is why displaying a News feed in different ways across the site is helpful. A link to the News section should be prominently displayed on the main menu for easy access.

If you are seeking to publicize events, whether they be online events (such as a hashtag selfie campaign or divestment campaign) or in-person events (such as a protest) having an Events page can be helpful.

There are different ways to organize and display Events. What I have done in the past is create a post category or tag called "Events" in which I post event information using a basic template (where I fill in the who/what/when/where/why/how) and include a link to the actual Facebook event page, if it has one. I also have a main menu link called Events that links to a page where the results for that tag or category are listed in one place. In the past, I have also displayed the Events as a category widget in the sidebar. Displaying events listings is not necessary, but it is effective in disseminating information as well as evoking a sense of action on the issue.

Understanding the WordPress Dashboard

The information I offer in this section is intended to give a general overview of the options that are available within WordPress. The information is accurate is as of November 2015, but it is subject to change as WordPress evolves. For the most up-to-date and comprehensive guide to learn about the Dashboard, visit the WordPress support page directly here: https://en.support.wordpress.com/start/

Updates

There are different elements of WordPress that will need to be "updated" to the latest releases. These include the following:

- Plugins
- Themes
- WordPress installation

Before updating, always make sure to make a backup of the site. It is important to keep your site updated with the latest versions of WordPress themes and plugins.

If you have a highly-customized site with several active plugins, keep in mind that sometimes they may not communicate well with each other and be "incompatible." Each product is a script written by someone different. Sometimes these plugins will not get along whether they are updated or not. But, when it comes to troubleshooting a WordPress site, any anomalies that appear are resolved through a process of elimination. When hiccups are encountered, one of the first steps that should be taken in diagnosing the site is making sure that all components are up to date.

Posts

Posts display the content (stories) you want to release to the world. They are displayed in the admin screen as a sortable list and can have particular categories and/or tags associated with them. Posts can be created, edited, or deleted via the Posts screen.

Media

The Media library is where all multimedia attachments are stored and managed. Any images, audio, documents, or video that can that be inserted into a post or page is automatically added to the media library. This includes images in JPEG or PNG as well as PDF documents and MP3 files (if any.)

Links

The Links section manages links to other websites that can be displayed as a widget. Sometimes this is useful and sometimes it is not, it depends on the intentions and overall goals of the community. However, "sharing is caring" in the virtual world. If a link to another site is shared on the website, you can possibly ask the other site to do the same for you.

Pages

Similar to the Posts screen, the Pages screen contains a sortable list of pages currently on the site. Pages should contain static information such as an About Us and Contact Us page. Pages should contain information that does not need to be updated often.

Comments

The Comments section is where public comments on posts or pages are managed. Commenting can be turned on and off and can be set up to be used by the public or registered users. These options can be modified in the Settings page.

The decision on whether to allow comments (and the time required to manage them) should be considered in advance. Does public opinion matter on the website?

Appearance

The Appearance page is where visual front-end of the website can be customized. This section includes several parts:

Themes

The theme is the overall look and design of the website. There are many themes to choose from in WordPress. Some are free and others are premium. Themes can control the front-page display, fonts, font sizes, and any special features they may offer, such as a streaming banner.

Once you find and select a theme, you should immediately create what is known as a "child theme" to retain any special coding or customizations that may be made to the theme CSS or PHP files (style and functions.) If a child theme does not exist and the developer of a theme releases an update for the "parent" theme, customizations could be overwritten. You run the risk of changes being wiped out after each update, which would require customizations to be made time and time again. This is unnecessary and can be completely avoided.

To quickly create a child theme, search for a highly-rated plugin in the Plugin screen. In the past, I have used a "child theme generator" called "Orbisius" but there are tons of others to choose from.

Customize

The Customize section controls certain aspects of the design such as color, fonts, and widgets. Click on this option to get a feel for what customizations are available for you. Some themes will offer more customizations than others. Additional customizations can also be found in Appearance > Theme > Theme options.

Widgets

Widgets are blocks of information that usually appear in the left and the right-hand columns of site pages. They normally provide links to other content on the site or on other websites. They can appear on all or a combination of specific posts or pages. The placement of information in sidebar areas should be planned and audited to see how effective they are in helping get specific information to site visitors.

Menus

Menus control the navigational structure of a website. Menus can be completely customized to point to any post, page, or link. They come in different styles and each theme will offer different ways to customize and display your menus. The website could have a "main menu" but also offer a menu with different options that will display somewhere else on site. Selecting the options you want displayed in your menu are easy to do via the Menus administration page.

Edit CSS

In the Edit CSS screen, you can customize the style of a theme by using CSS, (Cascading Style Sheets) which use shortcodes to control the styling of elements such as fonts or content headings, all at once.

Editor

In the Editor section, advanced users can view or edit the core PHP (PHP: Hypertext Preprocessor) files for themes and plugins. While it is not mandatory that one be fluent in PHP to manage a successful site, one can learn to work with PHP by searching for tutorials. One way to customize a theme or plugin without knowing much PHP is to go to the website of the developer and look through their FAQs and user forums for codes that may help you make specific modifications.

Plugins

Plugins are different "scripts" (codes) that give you different types of functionality on a website. Some are free and some are premium. There are many different types of plugins that can help with just about every creative process or display you can think of.

Sometimes building a WordPress website is like putting a puzzle together. If you do not have the pieces you need, there is a good chance that you will find a plugin somewhere that will give you the functionality you are looking for. Just remember that the more plugins you use, the greater chance you have of causing some sort of incompatibility issue. Plugins are created by different authors around the world and are not always guaranteed to work together perfectly.

Users

This section manages site users, which can be given different levels of access and permissions within the site. Users should be carefully considered. There are several user types in WordPress, which can be viewed here: https://codex.wordpress.org/Roles_and_Capabilities

Tools

The Tools section offers a series of different tools, including search engine verification and the ability to import/export blogs, database tables, and other information to and from other sites. I do not use this area, but advanced users might find it helpful.

Settings

The Settings section controls the general features of the site including the name, tagline, comment controls, and other general site specifications.

Why is content placement important?

The placement of content, imagery, subscription forms, and buttons is of critical importance. Here are a few golden rules that can help you:

- Make sure that the most important information and engagement options (take action buttons, social media links, and subscription fields) are displayed "above the fold" in the area that appears immediately when a web page is accessed (without having to scroll down.)
- Include social media sharing links at the bottom and/or top of each post to make it easy for site visitors to share information.

- Make subscription and sign-on buttons accessible so that folks can easily sign petitions or register to receive automatic updates. Your listserv network is your "cream of the crop" audience. These individuals are your followers who are interested in receiving automated notices when new posts are published. This particular audience needs to be cared for because they represent people that are ready to take action in solidarity.
- Make sure that the graphic design, color scheme, and overall look and feel correspond well with the movement. To diagnose and determine what areas can be improved, read through the Traffic and Quality Control section to learn how to gauge page traffic and statistics.

What are the key components of content?

There are a few key components of content (posts) that I try to keep in mind when publishing. The following questions can be helpful to ask yourself when developing and laying out content:

- What is the end goal of this message? To raise awareness? Or to stimulate someone to take action?
- Is truth being spoken or is fear being instilled?
- Are there any ways this piece of content can be set up to stimulate direct action?
- Are there links to additional resources?
- Does the content need to be translated?
- Are the conceptual basics covered? (The who, what, when, where, why, and how?)
- Is there anything left unsaid?

The purpose of each post can be different and the answers to these questions will also be different.

How often should you post?

Your posting schedule should be based on the needs of the community issue at hand. The more often you post, the more your audience expects to receive information. However, you should consult with the community and think critically about the posting schedule because sometimes developing a lot of content can be cumbersome...or unnecessary, as resources and people-power may be limited, or the movement might just need a static website that provides contact information instead of frequent posts. I have taken both approaches and have created static websites that serve as hubs to other websites or social media. I also have websites through which I actively create content and post weekly or every other week. It is really up to the community, the resources available, and the goals of the movement. Just remember that as you grow your website and audience that you are actually developing virtual relationships with other human beings at the other end of the screen.

You should consult with the community about a schedule as well as participation in the content development process. Content does not have to be text-based; it can also come in the form of audio, video, or pictures. The more multimedia you use, the more you can bridge across different social media platforms or multimedia networks to reach multiple worlds and expose your work to as wide an audience as possible.

How and why should you backup your website?

Backing up your site is critical, as updates or random changes can occur at any given time and cause your site to encounter errors. A plugin can be used to automatically create site and database backups on a schedule. I use the BackWPup free plugin to backup the site and database every day and email me any errors. There are free and paid options you can choose from to run backups, but I recommend this plugin as it has given me excellent results.

How do you make a website multilingual?

When I first created the Mission-Texas.com site, I made it bilingual by manually copying and pasting content from page to page, then translating it. Since the Mission site was created in the days before social media and WordPress, I had to do the best with what I had to make it happen, regardless of how cumbersome the process was.

But now that I use WordPress, there is an amazing plugin called WPML that I use and highly recommend. It makes websites multilingual in just a few clicks. It also offers administrators an easy-to-use interface that allows multiple users and translation management.

WPML offers free but a limited version that can help with basic post translations. But if the budget allows, purchasing the subscription for the full version is one of the best investments you can make on a digital resistance war front, especially if you have a multilingual audience. This plugin also offers fantastic customer service and guides to help. You can learn more about WPML here: http://www.wpml.org.

What are some ways to remain relevant as technology progresses?

The speed of technological development is incredibly fast, which can present different issues for digital warriors. For example, the methods I was using at the beginning of my journey are dramatically different from what I use now. However, there are a few things you can do to try and stay on top of the new technology and tech trends while being budget, time, and energy conscious.

1. Google search popular or new social media platforms so that you can automate publishing to them.
2. Routinely check out popular tech blogs for the latest tech trends.
3. Ask folks of all ages from the community for suggestions on new social media platforms or other digital tools.

CHAPTER 7: TRAFFIC AND QUALITY CONTROL

Why is self-reflection important in digital resistance?

Because the internet is always in motion, it is important to remain flexible and open to new ideas. Constant self-reflection or "quality control" is critical to creating a sustained increase in your audience and digital power. By regularly examining the statistics of the site, you can:

- Determine any keywords that are being used to find the site.
- See what posts or pages are the most popular.
- View the number of visitors referred to your website from different social media networks.
- Learn the demographics of your audience.
- Locate weak spots in your site visitor flow and rethink the placement of information.

What are web statistics and how can they be monitored?

There are different ways to use statistics on WordPress. One way is through a WordPress plugin called Jetpack that offers an entire package of functionality, including the ability to publish to social media networks and view live statistics. Once Jetpack is installed and activated, statistics can be viewed by selecting "Site Stats" from the Jetpack menu in the Dashboard.

Google Analytics offers another free and more advanced method to view statistics. You must have a Google account to connect to this tool. There are numerous in-depth tutorials available that teach how to use Google Analytics. Personally, I setup my Analytics accounts to email me every week. I also go into the account and snoop around to see what I find. I usually learn something new each time I do this.

Why are collaboration, cross-posting, and clickable logos important?

In the virtual world, sharing is caring. Being part of a network helps increase exponentiality, which is important to growing an audience. One way to reach new audiences is to collaborate with other digital warriors to share links to each other. Cross-posting does not necessarily need to be strictly text or articles; it could also be in the form of a widget link or logo that is inserted on another website.

Should statistics be made public?

I have gone back and forth with this question on different projects. In some cases, displaying the number of visitors may be an effective strategy to show the opposition that the movement is being felt across the world. This presents the movement as having some sort of public power, which is important when the community is lacking economic power or has problems getting media coverage.

Another way to share statistics is to allow social media share buttons (that appear below a post) to list the active number of shares. I started displaying social media shares on Xica Nation and Xicana Chronicles a year ago. What I have found is that different types of content goes viral on certain platforms versus others. This is good information to know and reflect upon, because it tells you whether a topic or theme is as popular as another, or if a certain social media platform is working (or not working) well for the site.

In the event that the website is not getting a lot of traffic, an audit of the statistics should be conducted and the digital strategy and/or layout may need to be revised. But do not be discouraged, low numbers do not mean that the website is not working. The fact that the website exists is a form of resistance in itself and can cause the opposition to take a step back.

Is it necessary to spend money to increase traffic?

Something awesome about rascuacha tech is that the more you get into it, the more creative your methods become. Your brain gets used to pushing beyond the limits of fear and low resources. There are many ways to share information in the digital world for free, so spending money is not always necessary in order to receive an increase in web traffic.

One option that I have been told works really well is Facebook advertising, which is in the range of about $20 but pushes your page to a huge audience and may be very well worth the money. But not every community has access to funds (even if it is just $20) so you should keep in mind what your limitations are so that you can work around them.

There are other free and organic ways to drive traffic to the website such as optimizing the SEO (search engine optimization) ranking of the site. Optimizing SEO makes the site and its posts rank higher on search engine queries, so taking the time to learn SEO can help drive more traffic to the site. I use the free version of a plugin called Yoast SEO, but there are many other plugins available. There are also plenty of free tutorials to learn more about how SEO can help the website.

PART IV: THINGS TO CONSIDER

CHAPTER 8: POTENTIAL OBSTACLES

Building a digital resistance warfront is a journey. There are many steps, angles, and details to consider in developing a successful site. Because the focus of this text is to support community-led movements, I will assume that access is limited to different types of resources. The following section will discuss things to consider and potential obstacles that may be encountered in digital resistance.

How many people are required to run a successful digital war front?

One obstacle I have often witnessed in digital resistance is a lack of participation and volunteer effort. There are many reasons for this that can include a lack of free time or stigmas around technology, particularly in communities where access to technological tools and know-how is limited. In cases where the technological divide in the community was large, I had to devise creative ways to incorporate feedback and opinions. However, a lack of participation should not necessarily be viewed as a bad thing. You must critically analyze the situation to see what is working or not working. For example, you may discover that because people are working full time they cannot lend themselves to participate in all meetings. Try to find creative ways to stimulate collaboration.

Is money a factor in a digital resistance campaign?

While the methods I outline apply to building a digital war front via a self-hosted (paid) WordPress site, please keep in mind that there are less expensive ways to create and run a successful virtual war front.

If a lack of money presents a problem, there is usually a way around it. This is where rascuacha tech comes into play. The lessons learned in poverty can play a pivotal role in the journey to overcome economic obstacles online. Con ganas, todo se puede armar. Do not let a lack of money get in the way of creativity.

Can digital resistance be compromised?

Those involved in social justice organizing may find themselves in touch with nonprofits and paid organizations that are also organizing and creating their own movements online. I have also witnessed a situation where these entities competed with the community for attention and resources. I call this phenomenon the "nonprofit industrial complex" and find that it is systemic. It is partially rooted in paid activists from privileged backgrounds who came into social justice "work" because they "want to help." They may never have had to defend themselves and their community for survival. Or maybe a non-profit is the recipient of a grant that may cause a conflict of interest. Sometimes the community's definition of what "justice" means and how to obtain it will differ with funded organizations and individuals. Certainly, there are good people that work within the machine, but that does not make the machine less harmful to community-led resistance.

Through End Family Detention, I found myself increasingly involved in conversations with nonprofits and paid activists. I also found myself in conversations with volunteer community activists and pro-bono lawyers as well as with detained mothers. Within the circles where paid entities existed, I very quickly became aware of power plays, hierarchal decision-making structures, and communication control. I witnessed the same -isms and ills I saw in society perpetuated within social justice organizing. It broke my heart and nearly discouraged me from continuing to participate. But it sparked me to take action and write this book so that other communities could assert themselves without having to compete for attention or resources.

What are the top five potential obstacles in digital resistance?

1. Spiritual vulnerability
2. Fear and self-doubt
3. A mindset of poverty
4. Burnout
5. Lack of planning

Spiritual vulnerability

It is imperative that a digital warrior be mindful of their spirit, of the energies that move through the digital world, and sentiments that move through them as they consume different types of digital information. The battle is as much inward as it is outward.

Fear and self-doubt

Do not let fear and doubt about the value of your individual contribution to the movement cloud any digital visions or creative ideas. Each digital contribution or act in solidarity makes the digital war front stronger.

A mindset of poverty

Thinking about all the things you and your community don't have can be overwhelming. Reflecting on your present economic situation negatively can get in the way of creativity. However, the grass is not always greener on the other side.

Make the best of what you have. Flip the script and try to use those things which are meant to oppress you, in your favor. I am not suggesting that you become complacent with struggling. I am suggesting that you keep the peace within yourself as you work through the struggle.

Burnout

The issue around which the community is organizing can be emotionally or spiritually heavy. Rest and take breaks when needed. Make the time to nourish your mind, body, and spirit to maintain optimal health.

Lack of planning

While some digital moves have to be made with very little time, it is critical to collectively plan the website, content, and outreach in advance as much as possible.

If the plan is not followed to the T, that is okay. At the very least, there will be an understanding of the purpose of the digital war front and where it needs to go. While one must be fluid with developments as they come, it is essential to have at least an outline of the vision. Otherwise, you run the risk of not making the most out of the limited resources, detracting from the mission at hand, or worse, putting the community at risk.

CHAPTER 9: SELF-CARE AS RESISTANCE

I wanted to end this book with some reflections on self-care as a form of resistance. I chose to insert this section at the end because I want this information to be the last thing on the reader's mind as they finish this book and begin their own digital journey. In no way should self-care be considered an after-thought or any less important than rascuacha tech or the work of digital resistance itself. I intentionally made this chapter short because I feel that the journey inward belongs to the individual. The *guerra florida* is different for everybody.

Why is self-care and preservation important?

As an individual from a community under attack, self-preservation and self-care are acts of resistance. Digital resistance is war...war on the mind, the body, and the spirit. A warrior must walk a path of self-preservation in order to continue the fight. This may include having to make some physical, spiritual, and perspective changes to ensure your optimal health.

What are some ways to take care of yourself during a digital resistance campaign?

The following list contains techniques that have helped me care for my physical, emotional, and spiritual well-being while engaged in digital resistance.

Physical

- Daily exercise. On some days I got for a 30-minute walk. On others, I like to follow a yoga/pilates workout video. My personal goal is at least 30 minutes of physical activity a day.
- When working, stretch at least once an hour to minimize work-related injuries.
- Take a 15 minute (minimum) walk in the AM and another in the PM.

- Use ergonomic keyboards, chairs, digital pens, and other tools. If possible, use computer glasses to reflect the glare of the screen during periods of prolonged exposure.
- Eat a healthy diet and get plenty of sleep.

Emotional

- Before you begin your work day, take the first five minutes of your time to see positive and life-affirming content online. It is important to train your mind to frequently experience positivity, laughter, and happiness so that it does not become overwhelmed with the negativity of the community issue at hand.
- Take mental breaks when needed. Do not feel guilty for stepping away from the machine for a little while to clear your mind.
- Talk to someone you trust or write in a journal to vent and release any thoughts that may be causing you negative emotional reactions. It is important to describe your feelings so that you can release them and keep moving forward in a safe and healthy way.
- Regularly schedule time for yourself to do something you enjoy. Allow yourself to relax.
- Practice forgiveness. It begins with you. It does not mean you will forget, but it does mean you choose to move on.

Spiritual

- Incorporate prayer, mantras, or some form of spiritual practice into your daily routine.
- Meditate.
- Dance.
- Seek spiritual guidance or make time to participate in spiritual ceremonies.
- Ground yourself in nature as often as possible to release thoughts, emotions, and any electric charges your body may have acquired through your contact with electronic devices. Take off your shoes and put your bare feet on the earth for several minutes. Envision any stress and negativity move downward and out through your feet and down into the ground so that earth can filter it and take care of it for you.

Regardless of the methods you choose to use to take care of yourself, the most important thing you can do is remain consistent. If you reach a point where you feel strong and healthy, don't let your guard down or change your positive habits. Stay focused and keep working to shine your light. Your strength contributes to the strength of the whole community. Be consistent in maintaining your optimal health. Know your limits, but reach for the stars.

BIBLIOGRAPHY

Forbes, Jack D. Columbus and Other Cannibals: The Wetiko Disease of Exploitation, Imperialism, and Terrorism. Seven Stories Press; Revised edition (November 4, 2008.)

ABOUT THE AUTHOR

 Iris "Tejaztlana" Rodriguez is a digital resistance artivist from San Antonio, Texas. Since 2002, she has engineered digital resistance movements for community-led justice campaigns using "rascuacha tech" to create budget-friendly online networks that boosts public awareness, create media buzz, grow action-oriented networks, and effect positive social change.

For the past 13 years, she has served as an organizer, multimedia producer, and digital warrior in community-led campaigns on issues such as environmental justice, family detention, decolonization, cultural arts, guerrilla media, Xicanisma, and public archives.

She is the founder of Xica Media, a Xicana-powered multimedia, multilingual network of six digital resistance channels (Xica Nation, Xicana Chronicles, End Family Detention, Mission Texas Coalition, Tezcatlipoca Records, and Yetlanezi) which have a collective following in over 120 countries, reaching all age brackets.

In 2014, she made internet history by publishing the first-ever online, interactive, community-curated altar for *Día De Los Muertos*.

Her digital works in the fight to End Family Detention have helped reach multilingual audiences across the world. She helped publish a trilingual resistance website in English, Spanish, and Tzu'tujil, a previously unwritten Mayan language. Through this effort, she also collaborated in the Visions From The Inside art project with CultureStrike, which was displayed at the United Nations in Geneva for one week.

She is a graduate of Mexican American Studies from the University of Texas at Austin.

www.ingramcontent.com/pod-product-compliance
Lightning Source LLC
Chambersburg PA
CBHW062051280526
45788CB00003B/1184